The Girl
Behind
the Wall

The **Girl** *Behind* the Wall

Elizabeth Barnes

J. Kenkade
PUBLISHING®

Little Rock, Arkansas

The Girl Behind the Wall
Copyright © 2017 by Elizabeth Barnes

J. Kenkade Publishing
6104 Forbing Rd
Little Rock, AR 72209
www.jkenkade.com
Facebook.com/JKenkade

J. Kenkade Publishing is a registered trademark.

Printed in the United States of America
ISBN 978-1-944486-71-6

This book recounts actual events in the life of Elizabeth Barnes according to the author's recollection and per-spective. Some of the identifying details may have been changed to respect the privacy of those involved.

The views expressed in this book are those of the author and do not necessarily reflect the views of Publisher.

Table of Contents

For my mother,
the bravest and strongest woman I
will ever know.
For the young women,
may you have courage and strength
to get through.

CHAPTER 1

Childhood Memories

I must say, I don't remember a lot from my childhood life, but I do know there were some good times and some bad times. Let's start with a good memory: the day we had my sixth birthday party.

You see, me and my cousin had the same birthday, so I didn't mind having our parties together and celebrating. We lived in Alabama at the time my dad was in the military, so we lived on post. We had everyone over and although my birthday is in December, it felt amazing outside—not too cold, so most of the kids were put outside.

You know how your parents would be if there were too many grown people and older people in the house? Kids would be out the door! I can't remember what gifts I got, but

I knew all of my family was there. My mom was pregnant with my baby brother at the time, so my aunts and 'gma' helped her with a lot.

What I remember most about my life from me being ten is that I lived with my mother in North Carolina. The things I mostly remember about North Carolina is the fair. When the fair came every year, my dad would take me and my baby brother Brandon too. He would take us to the park or Chuckee Cheese on other weekends.

Then one birthday, my mom forgot when I turned eleven.

Do you know how hurt I was?

I still give her a hard time to this day. Love you, Mom. No really, I know she was working hard for me and my brother and doing her best being a newly separated wife. North Carolinian schools were okay... I mean it was school. Right after my eleventh birthday, my mom decided she and I should move back to Alabama where all my friends and cousins were. I was more than happy! I knew this was gonna be great! What I didn't know was where we would be living. Of course, I figured with my grandparents and two uncles in their house where I originally grew up for a little while.

Well… a little while turned into like a year and a half: with living with my grandparents and two uncles, to living with my uncle, aunt, and my favorite cousins, to living with my other aunt, uncle, and my cousins who are like my baby sister and brother, to eventually moving in with my godmom. I didn't mind at all. I never felt alone and always had someone to talk to. Trips to the beach on the weekends when school was out was everything to me at this time. We eventually moved back in with my grandparents, but I didn't mind. Being the only granddaughter means you get spoiled.

We lived with my grandparents up until the time I told what happened to me.

CHAPTER 2

❧

The Worst Time in My Life

You ever had bad dreams? Does a certain smell or thing happen that ever reminds you of him? Them? No? Yeah, I didn't think so. I couldn't understand what was happening to me or why. All I knew was something wasn't right.

Should I tell someone?

Who am I going to tell?

For this was the third time something like this happened to me and I didn't tell the first two times, *so why would anyone believe me now?* I couldn't take it anymore, so I decided to tell everything that happened to me the next day. I decided to tell my mom, hoping and praying she would believe me. As I woke up that morning, I wasn't so sure I should mention anything.

I mean, why?

Everything was fine, but I knew if I didn't tell, they would be back. I walked to my mom, Paris, who was in the living room talking to her friend Fran. I politely told my mom we needed to take a walk and of course, just as I thought, my mom had the worried look on her face. Fran decided to join us.

As we turned the corner, I began to cry and Paris wasn't understanding why. Once I was calm, I revealed all the secrets I had been keeping in for two years.

I told my mother and Fran that I had been molested by not one, but three men and they were all family members.

Fran and Paris were both puzzled, stopped walking, and were both speechless. Once they could come to the terms of what they heard, Paris needed details and needed them now.

So, I started.

My first time and first person was with Geoff and it happened in the fifth grade. I decided to tell Fran and Paris everything including places and what happened.

So I started with this:

"I was supposed to be going to my program at school, but instead he made a detour and ended up at his house. Geoff walked me in, made me lay on his bed, and pulled my panties down as he pushed himself inside of me. I felt the tears rolling down my eyes. Instead of letting them fall down my cheeks, I sucked it up and did what I thought I had to do."

When Geoff was done, he told me, "Don't tell anyone cause it's gonna hurt this family."

Of course, I kept my mouth closed.

Geoff finally took me to the program and I cried the entire time. Once the program was over and I saw my friends, I acted as if nothing happened.

The second time it happened with Geoff, I stayed the night over my cousin's house. Of course nothing would happen; I mean...everyone was there, but I was wrong once again.

I woke up to pee and the next thing I know, as I was washing my hands, the door opened. I didn't think anything of it except one of my cousins must've gotten up too.

Nope. It was Geoff coming in with his hand over his mouth as if he was shushing me to be quiet. He cut off the lights and told me to not wake anyone up or make any loud sounds. He told me he knew this is what I wanted, but that's not what I wanted at all.

What I wanted was to run…run far away, but to where?

I wanted Geoff to stop.

He was done in five minutes, but it felt like a lifetime to me. He told me to wash up before I went back to bed and to be quiet, so I did just as he asked. I went back in the girls room and said not a single word. Instead, I laid there crying.

Fran and Paris were disgusted from what they heard, but needed to know who else.

I continued with my second molester and although he never inserted his penis inside me, I still felt nasty inside. I proceeded to tell them that the second person was even closer than Geoff was to me—it was Mark.

Paris said, "Mark? How?"

I said, "When you are young, you're told to listen to your elders and do what's asked of you, and that's exactly what I did. He would wait for my grandma to leave and go to the store and have me close all the doors and cut on the air conditioner to make it appear that's why the doors were shut. Then he would make me get a chair out and pull my pants off. After he made me stand on the chair, he would lick my vagina."

I felt so nasty just saying those words. It made me want to stop, but I knew I had to tell everything like I did with Geoff. The last one was the worst. Fran and Paris were silent for a minute, but after I told them the name of who was next and last,

Since it wasn't my first time seeing one, I basically knew what he wanted from me, but what I didn't know was Todd had more in mind for me and my body.

they were ready to hear what he did. They both had a serious look on their faces. I started with the last one—Todd. What he made me do and did to him was sickening and he was not even a close family member.

I started off with how I would go down to Todd's mom's house and ask for things my grandmother needed, and Todd would be there instead of Lily, her grandmother's friend. Todd would show me his penis and put my hand on it. Since it wasn't my first time seeing one, I basically knew what he wanted from me, but what I didn't know was Todd had more in mind for me and my body.

First, he would make me come to his room in case someone came home. He would make me touch and suck his penis until he came in my mouth.

What's worse is he wouldn't let me spit it out, so I had to swallow his sperm.

After a week or two of going down to Lily's house and he was home alone, I knew the routine.

But today was different.

He wasn't alone and he still made me do things to him, but he took me to the woods and decided to rape me instead. Of course… no one was near. Even if I screamed, no one would hear me. All I could think about was,

Why me?

Was it something I wore?

The way I looked?

How could my grandmother not know I'd be gone for 45 minutes to an hour and not be looking for me?

I told Fran and Paris I attempted suicide plenty of times, but never succeeded. Everyday I felt like dying. Fran and Paris comforted me and apologized for not being there and told me they will fix this. For some reason, I felt bad for all three men and didn't want them to go to jail, but why should I care about their lives after what they did to me?

When they got back in the house, my grandmother Ruth asked Paris what was wrong with me.

Paris smiled and said, "Nothing, she's okay. Aren't you Destiny?"

I looked at my grandma and said, "Yes, ma'am."

I couldn't understand. I felt bad for the families I would tear apart and the men, but I knew I didn't want them to be hurt, so I pleaded with my mom to just let them be.

The evidence was gone and it was my word against theirs. To this day I don't know why we never went to the police station or whether it was my pleading or what. As we got home, Paris talked to me and told me that she was going to send me off to live with my grandmother in Mississippi for a couple of months.

I was not happy at all and once again blamed myself for talking. I questioned myself so many times of why I told. *Now I have to leave, but why should I leave? I did nothing wrong.*

Paris explained to me that it is not my fault and right now Paris couldn't keep me safe right then. Two weeks had passed by and

Paris was trying to prepare me for what was about to come. I was about to be moving thirteen hours away to a small town in Mississippi to live with my other grandmother, Jeanie. It was the middle of my sixth grade year and I was not ready to meet new people or leave my best friend Brittany behind. At that time, I didn't know it was for my own good. On Friday at 5 a.m., Paris told Destiny that they would drive up. Paris could stay until late Saturday, so I wouldn't feel too bad.

Beep, beep, beep.
The 4 a.m. alarm went off on Friday morning and it was time to get up, get dressed, and hit the road. Paris packed the car the night before, so all we needed to do was stop and grab breakfast. I, who was still not understanding, decided not to talk to Paris the entire trip so I could show Paris how I was feeling. Little did I know, Paris was hurting deep inside, not just for me, but for herself too.

This was by far the best and worst thing Paris had to do…leave me, her baby in a place eight hours away, but in a place she knew would be safer than where she was. Paris decided to stop half-way through the trip so she and I could talk over lunch. She knew I was mad at her, but she needed me to know why she was doing this and who she was doing this for.

"Destiny… I want you to know that I love you so much, and for me to have you at such a young age was hard on me. But right now, as a mother, I am not protecting you as I should and leaving you with your grandmothers is the best thing for you right now. I need you to understand this," Paris said.

I was crying saying, "Mom, you're making it seem like it's me that's in the wrong when really all I did was speak up. Was I wrong to tell you? Should I have just let it go? I understand why you have to do this. I just don't get why you make me feel like I had to leave for the situation to get better!"

Since Paris knew exactly how I was feeling, she could explain more on the rest of the trip. We went ahead and stopped for gas as well. *Now back on the road with four more hours to go.* Paris decided it was time to talk and explain herself to me.

"Destiny, I never wanted you to feel less than the young woman you are. The reason I want you to leave is for me and you. I feel safer knowing you're safe. I know the situation won't change with the men, but I do know that while you're gone, my plan is to make bigger plans for the both of us. The living situation we're in will be different and I will be home more. I hope you understand everything I am doing is for you?"

I turned to Paris with tears in my eyes and said, " I understand. I just wish it wasn't under these circumstances."

Paris, with tears now running down her face said, "I know baby. Me too."

We decided to enjoy the rest of the trip with music and laughs. We arrived in Jackson, Mississippi around 4:40 p.m. at Paris' mother-in-law Jeanie and grandmother Mae's house. Both Paris and I, tired from the road trip, bought all of my belongings in, showered, and laid on down for the night.

CHAPTER 3

❧

The Stay at Grandma Jeanie's House

Sizzle, Pop, Pop! The sound and smell of bacon flowed through the house as grandmother Mae Jean was cooking homemade biscuits, bacon, eggs, pancakes, and grits for the girls. I yawned, rolled over, and looked at Paris. I tried to make a photogenic picture in my head of my mom and how she smelled, smiled, and even as far as the fine line wrinkles in her skin, for I knew Paris was leaving later on tonight and I didn't know for how long, unfortunately. Paris opened her eyes and woke up to my face staring right at her. She knew what was going on. So instead of moving, she just laid there and did the same thing. Five minutes later, we both were up, out the bed, and had cleaned up for breakfast.

"Oh how I've missed these home cooked meals, said Paris," as she got back up for more pancakes.

"Destiny," said Paris. "Later on we will go do some school shopping and get you enrolled for school before I leave tonight."

I was still pissed she was leaving me in the first place, so I just nodded my head. Right after breakfast, Paris decided it'd be best if we go ahead and enroll me in school, and get shopping out the way so she could get a little rest before leaving.

We went to the mall, got clothes, shoes, and after that, we went to Walmart for snacks and extra food in the house since Paris didn't know how long I would be there.

We ended up getting done with everything around 4 p.m. Paris decided to have one last sit down with me and have a talk with me about what she expected of me and why she was doing what she was doing. Of course, I was not ready to acknowledge that my mother was actually leaving me. I had no choice but to listen. I knew I had no choice and I would make my mother proud. I ended up crying when Paris left for two days and it wasn't because I didn't know when she was coming back, but because I missed her so much.

I ended up meeting the kids next door, Albert and Courtney. They were close to my age and treated me okay. I even got into my first fist fight there only three weeks after being there and Courtney was there to help me.

I learned Spanish!

I even had more friends from school and church whom I stayed the night with and went over to their house. I still talk to two of them from time to time. Paris and I talked everyday up until the day Paris came back. Paris came to get me as soon as school got out for the summer. I was ready to get back to my friends and family.

CHAPTER 4

❧

The Return Home

Wen we got back, Paris even had a new man and a new place to stay. We lived up the street at TT's house. Not knowing if I should always have my guard up, I decided to have a talk with Wayne and let him know the "rules" when dating my mom. *Lol.*

Of course at thirteen, what can I really do?

I found out Wayne was exactly what my mom and I needed to complete our family.

We went on trips to the beach. Not only did we go, but Denise, Alan, and Andrea went as well. So, it made me feel great knowing I had someone to play with. We even took a family trip to Wild Adventures with Brandon too and spent the entire weekend riding rides, seeing animal shows to even riding the train around to see all the other animals. I even admired him more than my biological father.

I mean, what girl wouldn't?

This is exactly what I had been dreaming about since I was a little girl—family vacations and trips. He was there for me and loved me like the princess I always dreamed I was.

Wayne was there for my surprise thirteenth birthday party which only my true friends and family showed up to, but that's okay. I was just happy to have people show up. About a month or two after my birthday, Wayne, Paris, and I went to live with my aunt who wasn't too far from my grandparents. I shared a room with my cousin, but it was more like having a sister. I even had friends over.

My biological father was there, but he wasn't there.

My seventh grade crush would get dropped off and stayed over for a little bit.

I must say, seventh grade seemed to be the best grade ever! From having all my friends together, riding the bus, seeing my first ever bus fight to having my first ever "boyfriend".

My mom and Wayne even took us on our first bowling date! When I went to Dauphin, I changed boyfriends and started talking to the "ugly boy from up the street" as Wayne called him. We went to the movies together, junior high school dances, and even stayed up late nights on the phone. The good life that is. A couple months later, Wayne and Paris found us a nice home. I finally had my own room!

This was the life— that is up until the day Wayne left.

He was there for three years of my life, and the day he left to move on was heartbreaking to me.

He of course gave me his number and told me to always call him when I needed him and he would be there. I called a couple times, but I never got a return call back. So, I just left it alone. I still had a dad there who was also my brother Brandon's father. I just always felt like the step-child instead of his! Not that he mistreated me or anything.

I just didn't feel the connection when I was younger. My biological father was there, but he *wasn't there* meaning we lived in the same city and I rarely saw him.

I don't have many memories of him except this one summer: I went and stayed with him and ended up meeting my other siblings which were three sisters and another brother. I also met his wife. I made some new friends and had a good time, but he once again was there *but wasn't*. He worked a lot and since I was thirteen, I was able to stay there by myself. His wife took me places when she had the time, but it still seemed like he wasn't there. I truly didn't start spending time with my biological father and his side of the family until I got married.

I have a wishy washy relationship with him to this day. I call him when it's needed; he is not the typical grandparent, which means he doesn't babysit or get his grandchildren like my dad, step dad, and mom. He has however been more involved in his grandkids' life since my baby sister has grown up and wanted them around. My siblings rarely speak to him. I'm sure it's the same reason I didn't and rarely do now which is from the lack of being there when I needed him the most.

CHAPTER 5

Teenager to Young Adult

School was coming back around the corner which meant homework, parties, and more homework. I never got in any school fights which was a good thing for me, but I got into some trouble from bringing home bad grades to going to the principal's office for not listening to teachers.

My ninth grade year—I will never forget one day, the day of 9/11.

I was in my homeroom teacher's class. Mrs. Burns and the principal were over the intercom talking and all of sudden, she saw the T.V. She saw the people running from the building, and the entire class was quiet. I mean…what words could be said? We had a moment of silence and went on about our normal school day. Moving on to the tenth grade was amazing—going to the High School becoming a Wildcat!

My sophomore year, I went in: I focused on school and playing sports. I got the focus on the school part somewhat right until I met my new boyfriend, Dwayne.

Things went from great to *uh-oh*.

I didn't think there would be a hiccup on the way, but when you skip school and have unprotected sex, what else should I expect?

The hiccup was a beautiful baby girl named Nova whom I had when I was sixteen. I was so scared to tell my mother. I took three tests at Dwayne's house and decided to tell Paris I needed birth control when in actuality, I was scared to tell Paris I was pregnant.

So, Paris made an appointment for me at the health department and that's when she found out I was three months pregnant. That was the day I knew I crushed all my mama's dreams for me. She cried so much and didn't speak a word on the drive home. I even over-heard her calling all my aunts and them telling her it was gonna be okay because we had family to support us. She called me into her room and told me everything was going to be okay. Since it was just Paris and me, I knew I would have to work after school to provide for Nova because Paris couldn't do it all.

I got a job at McDonalds, my first job ever! While I worked, Paris and my family and friends helped with taking care of Nova. I knew I had to do something for my child and my life, so I joined the military my junior year going into my senior year. After having Nova, I knew

I decided to tell Paris I needed birth control when in actuality, I was scared to tell Paris I was pregnant.

I needed to have a plan for our future, so I went off to Basic Training when Nova was six months which was my junior year of high school, going into senior year. I was so scared leaving her behind, but I knew she was in good hands. I spent nine weeks training and making new friends.

This was one of the most scariest experiences in my life! The first day of basic training, they had us up at like 3 a.m., and we were in front leaning rest position for what seemed like a lifetime, but I'm sure it was only like 20 minutes. Every where I turned, there were girls in tears whether from fear or being tired.

For me, it was pure fear and me thinking, *"What the hell did I just get myself into?"* I must say though, after the first week, it got better and I met a lot of new friends whom I call sisters now. I learned a lot about myself! Family day was so much fun. We went to the water park, had a picnic in the park and had dinner all before having to take me back before 18:00 hours. I even had Denise, Dwayne, and my other cousin come to my family day and graduation when my mom, dad, my brother, aunt, daughter and grandmother came!

Graduation was amazing!

Hearing my name called out and knowing everyone who loved me was there and supporting me was amazing! I left Nova's dad when I got back and decided to focus on Nova, school, and work.

It wasn't easy being a single parent, but I had a lot of support from my best friend, Brittany her family, and my own family. One day, while traveling to drop Nova off at daycare which was down the street from the house, we got into a minor but scary accident. Nova was only like seven or eight weeks old, and a man came up flying from behind not paying attention and smashed right into us! I was so scared. All I could do was blow the horn, ter-rified Nova was hurt. I didn't want to move. The daycare worker came out and ended up calling my mom and the police. She checked on Nova for me and she was fine. I ended up going to the hospital just for precautionary reasons. I was fine. I don't think I told Nova's dad. *Oh well, he knows now!*

When I got back, I decided to stay fo-cused on school, military, and Nova, especial-ly knowing that friends and family who said they would be there to help my mom with Nova failed me.

Meeting Chris:
I met Chris in my senior year of high school. We both worked at the same fast food restau-rant—McDonalds, duh! We started off as friends and then soon realized after talking that we both had the same dreams and vi-sion for our kids. It all started out with a few kisses here and there as he came in my drive-thru. But I knew Chris and me would be a lot more than just coworkers and friends. I knew I wanted to spend my life and build a family with him. To make things even better, his mom and I got along great! She was my

manager and she adored me and my daughter Nova.

As soon as I became the girlfriend, things seemed to change between us.

You know when you're with someone and get to know them and then all of a sudden, you notice they don't speak to you like they used to?

When they see you or they don't call or text you like they used to… yeah thats what I noticed between Maria (Chris' mom) and me.

Chris was different from all the other guys I dated. Aside from him being white, he had dreams and goals. That was the motivation I needed to do what I had to do, not only for Nova, but for myself as well.

Paris was fond of Chris. She liked him more than she liked Dwayne, so that's a plus.

Paris decided she wanted to do something more with her life since I joined the military, so she decided to join as well. I know right? Only my mom.

I was so proud of her for going for what she wanted, but where would that leave Nova and me?

While Paris was gone off to basic training, a tornado came through my high school killing eight students and one lady.

That was the scariest day of my life and I'm sure it was worse for the students who were hurt and had friends pass away because of this tornado. I ended up staying with Chris for the next two nights. Paris, who should have been more concerned for me and my safety, was more pissed that I was staying at Chris' house and not my grandmother's house. You see, Paris had a plan, but I had my own little plan.

Chris and I talked about Paris going off to BCT and Chris told me I could stay there until after my senior year. Then we would get a place together, get married, and wait until I got stationed. Paris, on the other hand, made arrangements for me to keep her car, live with my grandparents, still go to work, and check in from time to time with details of what was going on when she called back home. I listened to some of that and I probably should have listened to my mother because it was not even a year of Paris being gone for basic combat training, annual individual training, and getting a duty station of Korea when I was once again pregnant.

No, it wasn't planned, but at least I felt like I

was a little bit more ready for this baby.

I felt like having Nova and having Chris there is what made it somewhat better. I felt a little less fearful of telling my mother this time around that I was pregnant not because she was in another country, but because I knew I had Chris and we were a family. I still had my military career and was still gonna pursue going active duty. That is… until the unit I was in got deployed to Iraq. Since I hadn't been to AIT, I couldn't go even after the baby. The unit decided the best thing to do was to medically discharge me out, but promised after the baby and after I go to AIT that I can still get back in and go active duty. I had a baby boy early November whom I named Kayden. I still worked at McDonalds and had already finished school, so the only thing left was to go back and start my career.

I felt a little less fearful of telling my mother this time around that I was pregnant… because I knew I had Chris and we were a family.

But I just couldn't leave my babies.

Plus three months later, Chris ended up finding out he would be getting deployed the next year, so what was the rush?

I decided to hold off and just stay home with the kids and work part time. I found another job working at the local grocery store in town while the older two kids were in school. My grandmother and aunts helped watch the baby. We found a three bedroom house to live in until he came back. It all worked for a while until Chris left. Everything was going good until I had family needing to borrow money and family wanting to stay over at the house to eat all my food. I wanted to say something, but I enjoyed the company of an adult. Chris found out the lights got cut off from Paris who was also over in Afghanistan and he was pissed!

The light bill was seven hundred dollars. Why? Because I was handing money out left and right to family like an ATM, partying every weekend or getting my hair and nails done on the regular (which by the way, I never did, but on special occasions). I had turned into someone else, but who?

ELIZABETH BARNES

Watching Chris Leave

When Chris was leaving for overseas, the family was able to spend the last night and day with him before he got on the bus. I'm not gonna lie… it was the most crushing/memorable times we spent. Crushing because he was leaving for a year and no one knew if he would make it back or not. Memorable because it seemed like we had the best conversation and sex ever! The ride home was horrible. I was in tears while trying to drive. The kids were everywhere in the back seat. I even had to pull over for a little bit to get the kids back in order and calm myself down.

CHAPTER 6

❧

Young Adult to Adult

Sometimes I wonder where I would be if I would've stayed in the military and went active? Would I be married?

Would I still have two children?

I don't know and I know you shouldn't think about the past, but look forward to the future. I should be pleased at the outcome I'm in. I mean, I was once a dancer for a couple months and that turned my family upside down. My parents were feuding with my husband all because they thought he wanted me dancing. I wanted to do it after not being able to get a job. Dancing seemed like the only job I could get, plus the money was good. I must say though, I'm glad I quit when I did because two months after I quit the club I was in, a dancer at got shot up by a customer and I saw it as a sign from God.

My future doesn't look clear and clean like how I envisioned it when I was sixteen and eighteen. I had more dreams for my babies and me. I had goals in my life that will never be.

What are my new goals you ask?

That's it… I don't know what my new goals in life are. I used to hate my job because I had to work second shift which meant I went to work when they were just about to get out of school and stayed until after they went to bed. So, I really only saw them in the mornings or on Sundays when I was off.

Now I work part-time in Nashville and have every weekend with my babies. I work to provide and give them everything they need and want. I did want a different life when I was younger.

What kind of life did I want you ask?

Well I envisioned myself two ways: either active military coming home around a decent time while putting my children to bed every night taking more vacations and more family trips together. I want my children to see the world more than I have seen it anyway. The second way was as an OB/GYN nurse—yes, labor and delivery!

I have loved babies since I was little and I see my daughter, Nova, has taken on that role as well. I hope she keeps that goal of becoming a nurse as I will stand behind her in every way. I hate not being here for her every day and not knowing how she really feels, if she's still being bullied or if she still wants to kill herself. No child should ever want to do that. When it's your own child, you have to ask yourself if your parenting skills are there and if what you're doing is right.

What should I do?

Can I really help her?

I just hope and pray that the modeling agency helps her confidence in every aspect she needs. Kayden, my son on the other hand needs more discipline. I should be more hard on him like I am with Nova, but I can only blame myself once again.

I "baby" him a lot.

I know I have failed my children and I know I have to make it up to them, but how? I wonder what my life would've been like had I gone active duty. Would I have more time to be with my kids, or would it be the same for them and me if I were to get deployed? Where would I be in my life right now? I guess I'll never know any of this, but where do I go and look forward to in the future?

For some reason, I always knew or felt my life would be complicated from being sexually abused by three close family members. Why wouldn't it be? Lol. I'm sure you're wondering why the hell I'm laughing at this situation, but the thing is, I forgave all these men a long time ago. I guess I watched so many Disney movies that I started seeing myself as the princess, even though my biological father was nowhere around and my dad was either busy or we never did any father-daughter things. That's why I preach to Chris about doing so much in Nova's life right now. It's so she will always feel that sense of being a princess and know how she should be treated as a young lady.

CHAPTER 7

A Second Trial in My Life

Knock *Knock* (at the door). I know we were not expecting anyone because I had just picked up Chris from the airport. I opened the door and it was the police.

"Ma'am, we have a warrant for your arrest."

"But… how can that be?

I told you the truth last week when you questioned me officer."

Clink Clank.

The cuffs were put on me. *They're taking me to jail, but for what?*

"For abusing your step-son," they said.

They said they had all the details and they had witnesses of how it all went down, but *do* they? *How? Who? Why?*

"Why would someone do this to me?
Who would say such a terrible thing?
How could Chris let this happen?
Am I going to be put in jail doing 10 to life?
Are they serious?"

Here's how it all happened:
We were at the jail and I was getting my fingerprints done. They're telling me to turn left, right, and look straight. But, I'm still confused about everything. They put me in a cell and told me I could get a phone call in the morning before court. I cried all night with no sleep at all. They gave me a flimsy mat to sleep on the floor with. *Shaking my head.* But all I could do was think about who would tell these lies on me and who would want me to suffer. I know a six year-old boy couldn't do this. I know he didn't like me because of his own personal reasons, but would he lie just to get his dad back? Would he put me in jail to have his dad back? I would hope not, but I was wrong… so wrong.

I knew I wanted to spend my life with him and build a family with him from living with my grandparents and uncles to living with my boyfriend and his family. I didn't mind the move at first because I was with Chris and we were a family. But a year and a half later in 2009, he was getting ready to deploy and it was time for us to be on our own; no more living with family.

I was alone at nineteen with three children ranging from the ages of two, four, and six with one at home, one in school, and one in daycare.

I loved the fact that he was going to be serving our country, but I hated the fact that he was leaving me for twelve months!

Of course I had lots of love and support from my family, but it still wasn't the same. Little did I know... everything would change and not for the better.

Once Chris was gone, it seemed like everything fell apart in my life in general. I decided to go to work part-time while the two oldest ones were in school and my grandma said she would help with the baby. No, I didn't have to work. I wanted to work. Of course I "okayed" it with Chris, and he was fine with it, but he also reassured me that me working was something I didn't have to do.

In my mind it was more of a "save money and bank it". Tell you the truth, I have no idea how I ended up not saving money and having to have Chris wire me money because I was being careless. One day while Chris was deployed, his oldest decided to tell his kindergarten teacher that he was being mistreated and this started up a big mess not only for me, but Chris as well. I tried my best to handle the situation, but some of Chris' family thought he needed to know how I was doing his child, and how I was behaving while he wasn't around. Chris called me angrily wondering what was going on and why I didn't tell him. All I could do was tell him the truth. I didn't think he needed to be concerned with any he/she say "bs".

Would he put me in jail to have his dad back? I would hope not, but I was wrong... so wrong.

He agreed and said he was coming home because he found out his son had been removed from the home. So instead of him coming home for good news, he had to come home because his family was trying to sabotage our relationship. I know what you're thinking... a six year old has no control over his actions, but you're wrong. For this six year old has control over a lot of things. He knows who he can and can not run over.

Once Chris was home, he decided to get everything straight and let everyone know I would never do such a thing. His main goal was to get Marlon back in our home. At that time, I didn't want to put myself in a bad situation, but I also knew he needed to go back with a clear mind. So, I did what I thought was right. Little did I know, it would come to bite me in the butt later.

Chris went back a week later. Marlon was not in our home. Instead, he was at my step mom's house until the investigation was over. Fast forward four months later, Chris was home for good and wanted his entire family back under one roof. I was good with that because he was home. We learned there was no indication of abuse, so they let him come back with exceptions that we must do family therapy.

Fine… whatever.

We did therapy and took Marlon to his weekly psychiatrist visits. Chris decided since I was still working at the grocery store and he was home that I could get more hours because he wanted to get back in the feel of being home for a month or two. I didn't have any problem with letting him take care of the kids and the house.

After a month, Chris was ready to start back working, so he got a job with his mother at the gas station. But he was working third shifts. No, I didn't like it. But hey, money is money and he got a job. Chris had annual training or AT every year for the National Guard. He was close to leaving in two weeks. The only problem I had was, *do I stay home alone with Marlon or do I have people stay with me?* So, I had my baby brother stay with me. Little did I know that trouble was waiting for me. Marlon misbehaved with some family members, and they didn't want to have him stay at their house. I totally understood. On the day of April 13th, my life changed. I woke up and got Marlon dressed for school only to find him trying to commit suicide by strangulation. I, of course, stopped him.

I was scared at the same time.

I mean, what would make a child want to kill themselves?

I called the psychiatrist's office and the nurse told me take him to the hospital. I did and they told me they needed to call DHR.

Of course, now I'm back in the web of my life going downhill. I did everything right. I even asked him why he tried to kill himself. The hard part was knowing I was a partial factor in the reason why. Of course I had to tell Chris this time because there was no hiding it when he would come home Sunday and wouldn't see his son.

Chris called his mom and had her meet me at the hospital so DHR wouldn't take Marlon away. When he got home on Sunday, he would go see him and he would get things straightened out Monday. Of course I was allowed zero contact with the child. Sunday came around and Chris was back home. Monday came and the police were at my door. I was being arrested for Aggravated Child Abuse. In the end, I was charged with Reckless Endangerment.

I had to pay court costs and court fees all for what?

Miscommunication?

This not only hurt me mentally, but physically.

I lost my job and couldn't get another one for a year and a half. We lost our apartment

ELIZABETH BARNES

we were living in and really had some rough times. Even our friends had given our kids Christmas gifts, not because they felt sorry for us, but because they knew our situation and they were able to give. I thank them for this every time I see them and tell them my goal is to pay them back.

52

CHAPTER 8

❧

Friends Come and They Go

I ended up losing a close friend this year because of my situation and being around Marlon. She couldn't have her life in jeopardy which I couldn't understand then, but now I see it from her point of view and only wish she had done the same for me!

I do want to thank her for showing me her true colors and letting me know who my real friends are.

I hope this book finds her one day and it gives her an insight into my world.

I hope she sees how looking in from the outside is exactly what she was doing. She stopped talking to me when I needed her the most. That's the part that hurts the most to me in all of this. Especially since she's like a sister to me.

I'm not the one to blame.

I'm not at fault, yet I always feel like I'm the failure.

Even though I was the one who suffered the most through this time. From not being able to provide for my family to preventing me from getting jobs.

These were all consequences I had to live with.

I said I was going to let it go and I am. This book is me doing just that, starting a new chapter for my family. Marlon is a teenager now and he needs everyone in his life who is going to support him and treat him the right way.

I will do what a mother is supposed to do when raising a son and raise him with the help of his father and the help of his grandmother. I will treat him like the son he is to me.

CHAPTER 9

Going Home Grown

You know going home as an adult is scary for me? I still get a funny feeling from the experiences of being raped, especially going home alone. I still have nightmares, I still jump in my sleep, and sometimes I burst into tears because I think of everything I've been through and how I have to protect my children.

I think about how these men are walking around freely and I can only blame myself for not speaking when it happened.

I never want my daughter or son to feel that pain of not being able to tell me anything, especially something *that* major. I always want them to know I will be the protector for them when no one else will be. I will always have their back. I know Chris is never going to let anything happen to me, but he's not always around and I have to defend myself or not put myself in those situations. I am grown and still feel alone most of the time. No one knows exactly what I'm going through and the pain I feel daily. I prayed for forgiveness and did, *but praying to get my sanity back is harder than I thought.* What more can I do?

CHAPTER 10

❧

New Beginnings

This will be a learning experience for the rest of my life, and I won't let anyone or anything come in my way again. I am in a much better stable place now and have no plans of ever going back to my old habits or ways. I have a strong support system on my team and I know they won't steer me wrong. I am excited about this new journey with my family! I plan on moving into our new house in the next year or so and having friends and family up from Alabama to celebrate my new life and a new beginning. I see dreams coming true not only for me, but for my family too. I hope to open up a community building where young ladies can be mentored and have a sense of being important in a single-parent family home or a two-parent home. I want to mentor young ladies who have been abused verbally or physically, and hopefully young men as well. That's my biggest goal in all of this.

My Inspirational Quotes

"Sometimes making yourself HAPPY is the best thing you can do for YOURSELF!"
-Elizabeth B.

"What they see as successful isn't how YOU see successful. Don't confuse the two."
-Elizabeth B.

"Never be afraid to tell the TRUTH! For you never know who it can help one day!"
-Elizabeth B.

"Never let THEM stop you from reaching the mountain top!"
-Elizabeth B.

"Go hard for what you believe in!"
-Elizabeth B.

"Just because you can't see what I'm going through doesn't mean I'm not going through something."
-Elizabeth B.

ABOUT THE AUTHOR

ELIZABETH BARNES goes by the name Michelle and is married to her high school sweetheart Joshua, who is in the military and also works at the Nissan Plant in Smyrna. She is the mother of three kids: two boys and one girl and they have one dog. Elizabeth was born and raised in Enterprise, AL, a small town right outside of Dothan, AL. She is a momma's girl and currently works for a health and beauty company. Her daughter models for Barbizon, a modeling and acting agency. Her stepson lives forty-five minutes away from her and her biological son is preparing to play sports. Elizabeth currently lives in Murfreesboro, TN.

J. Kenkade
PUBLISHING®

Also Available from
J. Kenkade Publishing

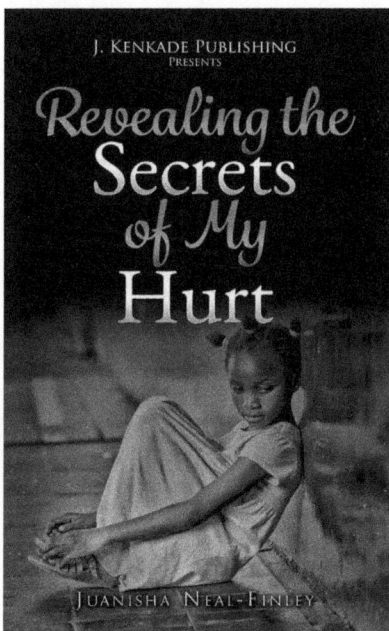

ISBN: 978-1-944486-13-6
Purchase at www.jkenkade.com

Captivating. Step into the life story of a young girl tormented by an abusive family. Young Cindy rewrites her experiences with a mother introduced to drugs, sexual abuse from her father, and death. Cindy reveals how strong God can make anyone in the midst of Satan's schemes. Experience her journey in "Revealing the Secrets of My Hurt."

Also Available from
J. Kenkade Publishing

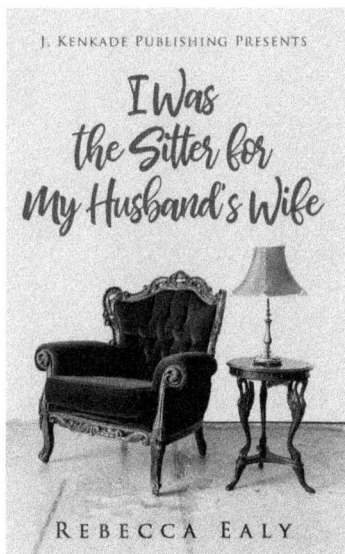

An engaging story about a single woman living far away from her family. Rebekah finds herself needing more fulfillment in her life as a nurse. She has been praying to God for her need until one day, He finally answers in the form of two strangers who aren't really strangers at all.

Available for purchase at www.jkenkade.com
Paperback 978-1-944486-17-4

Also Available from
J. Kenkade Publishing

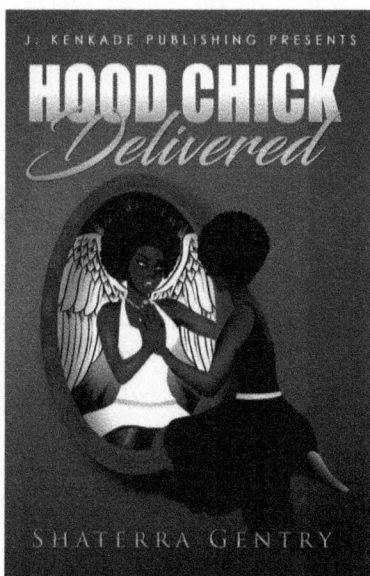

Hood Chick delivered describes a woman's troubled past as she is introduced to stripping and violence. After a friend gets shot and put into a coma for a few months, Layna cries out unto God, who tells her to commit to a life of Christ so that her friend may be saved. This novel describes a life that falls into submission with God, after a life of defiance with the devil.

Available for purchase at www.jkenkade.com
Paperback 978-1-944486-16-7

www.ingramcontent.com/pod-product-compliance
Lightning Source LLC
LaVergne TN
LVHW041207080426
835508LV00008B/839